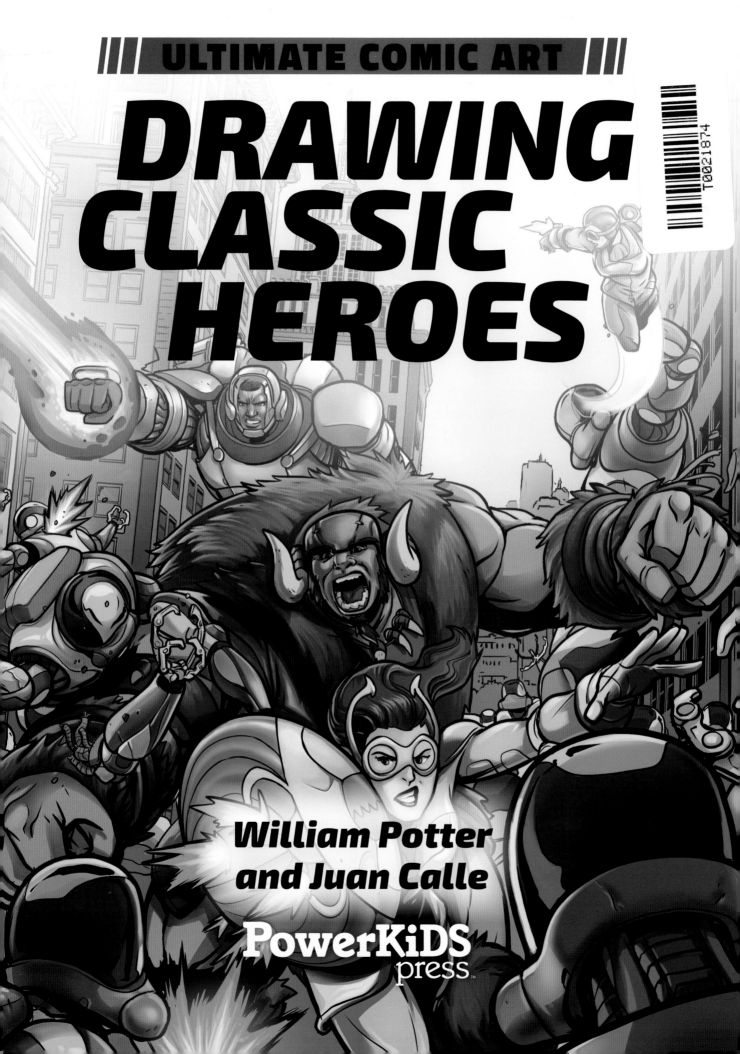

DRAWING CLASSIC HEROES

**William Potter
and Juan Calle**

PowerKiDS
press

CONTENTS

CREATING COMIC HEROES

Comics are a fantastic way of sharing stories. Whether your tales are personal or packed with super-powered heroes and villains, we'll help you bring your wildest adventures to life!

STEPS AHEAD

We're going to focus on those comic hotshots — the heroes. Step-by-step instructions will show you how to draw convincing characters, with guides on anatomy, poses, costumes, and planning fight scenes. We'll lead you through the steps to completing your first comic book pages!

COMICS FOR ALL

Whether you want to draw comics just for fun or dream of becoming a comic book professional, this book is packed with ideas and guides to help you make up your own characters for incredible adventures. We'll show you how to bring your characters to life and give you the tools to create your own comic strips.

Capital City is under attack from a wave of hostile androids. Save it from destruction by uniting The Vigilant — the city's greatest heroes. Read on to discover drawing guides for these champions — and to invent your own fantastic characters!

GETTING STARTED

You don't need a desk full of expensive tools to start making comics. You just need a pen, some paper, and a wild imagination!

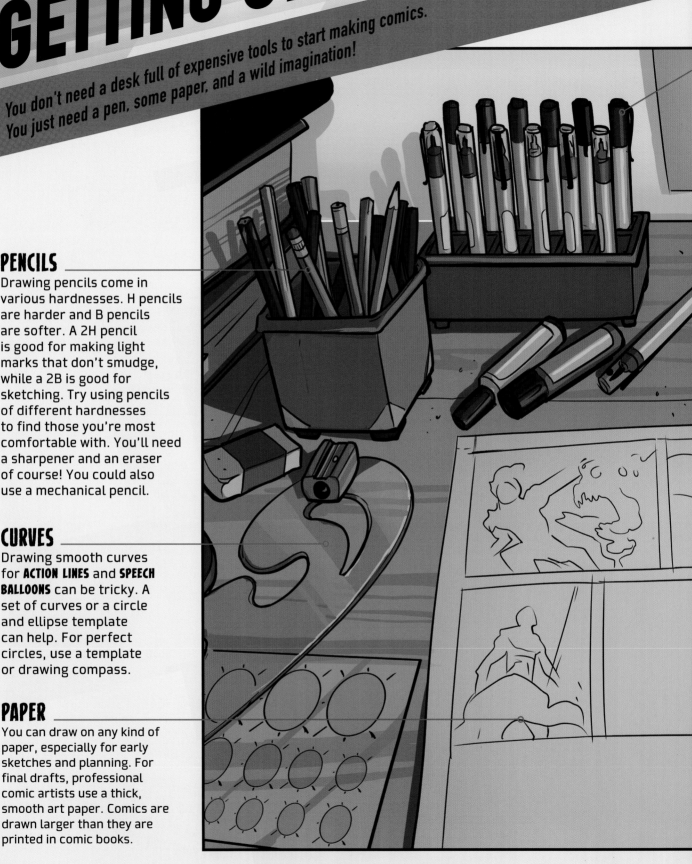

PENCILS

Drawing pencils come in various hardnesses. H pencils are harder and B pencils are softer. A 2H pencil is good for making light marks that don't smudge, while a 2B is good for sketching. Try using pencils of different hardnesses to find those you're most comfortable with. You'll need a sharpener and an eraser of course! You could also use a mechanical pencil.

CURVES

Drawing smooth curves for **ACTION LINES** and **SPEECH BALLOONS** can be tricky. A set of curves or a circle and ellipse template can help. For perfect circles, use a template or drawing compass.

PAPER

You can draw on any kind of paper, especially for early sketches and planning. For final drafts, professional comic artists use a thick, smooth art paper. Comics are drawn larger than they are printed in comic books.

PENS

Pens are a matter of personal choice. You might try out many different kinds before you find the perfect match. Find a pen that gives you a solid, permanent line. As you grow as a comic artist, you'll want to expand your pen collection. Eventually, you'll need pens of different thicknesses and a marker for filling in large areas.

BRUSHES, FOUNTAIN PENS

Inking over your pencils with a fountain pen or a brush dipped in ink will require some practice and a steady hand, but it can produce great results! A brush will give you more control over the thickness of your lines. Brushes are also good for filling in large areas with black ink that won't fade. You might also like working with brush pens.

STRAIGHT EDGES

You'll need a smooth metal or plastic ruler to draw comic panels and lines for comic book lettering. A triangle is also useful for panel drawing.

Many professional comic artists draw and color their art using tablets and computers. However, when you're just starting to learn and practice comic art skills, nothing beats good old pen and paper. You can get your ideas down while mastering basic techniques.

BODY MATTERS

When you can draw a figure with accurate PROPORTIONS, your characters will look more realistic. Superheroes and villains often have exaggerated muscular physiques — some may even have animal or alien features!

The human body is **SYMMETRICAL**, with the bones and muscles on the left matching those on the right.

Men's bodies are often wide at the shoulders and chests, then narrower at the hips. Women's bodies are often narrow at the waist and wider at the hips, like the number 8.

All human bodies are about eight heads tall. The waist is about three heads down from the top of the body, and the hands reach midway down the thigh.

TOP TIP
You don't have to give all of your comic book characters an athletic build. Use different heights and body shapes so that readers find it easier to tell them apart.

When you draw a person standing up straight, you should be able to draw a straight line from the top of their head down through their waist, to their knees, and through the center of their feet. Their shoulders should push out as far as their bottom, while their chest pushes out as far as their toes.

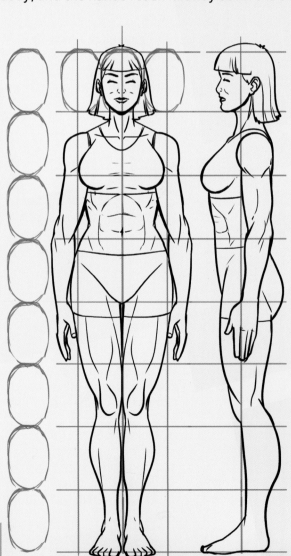

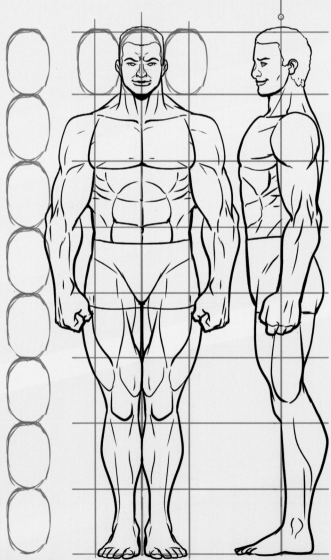

6

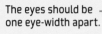

FACE TIME

Faces have their own proportions, with eyes and ears about halfway down the head. Here are average faces you can use for reference.

The ears are about the same height and position as the nose.

The eyes should be one eye-width apart.

Jaws are important to the shape of a person's face. They can be wide and square, narrow and sharp, or round and soft.

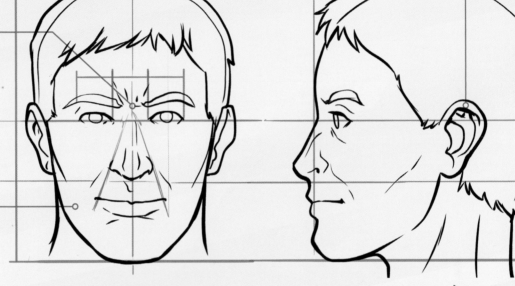

The nose forms an imaginary triangle with one point above the nose and one point on either side of the mouth.

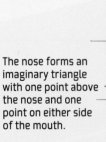

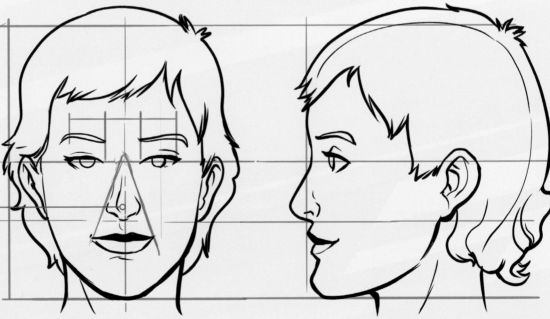

Look at your friends' and family members' faces. You will see many variations. Sketch the details you see and study their hairstyles. You can use traits like these to make each of your comic characters unique.

HEROES IN THE MAKING

What makes a great comic book superhero? Here are our design notes for four new characters, plus some guidelines on how you can use these principles for creating your own superheroes.

CHARACTER CONCEPT

What is the basic concept for your character? Mammoth is a hero from the Ice Age. He has a lot to learn about the modern day—not least, how to behave politely!

NAME: MAMMOTH

REAL IDENTITY: Grurrn

POWERS: Super strength, resilience, and fast healing.

ORIGIN: Grurrn is a super-strong hunter from the last Ice Age who was discovered frozen in a glacier. His powers come from an ancient mammoth god.

STRENGTH ◆◆◆◆◇
INTELLIGENCE ◆◇◇◇◇
SPECIAL POWERS ◆◆◆◇◇
FIGHTING SKILLS ◆◆◆◇◇

COSTUME

A hero's costume should logically follow from their character concept. Mammoth's costume gives him a wild and primitive look. The helmet is a reminder of his connection to the tusked mammoth god.

TOP TIP
You can find design inspiration in the past and the present. Golden Dart has a retro look based on a 1930s pilot, brought up to date with some modern tech.

MOTIVATION
Why does your hero choose to fight crime? Golden Dart is haunted by the loss of her mother. Many heroes choose to tackle villains after witnessing a tragedy, or to make up for a past mistake. Giving your character a strong reason for being a superhero will make them more compelling.

NAME: GOLDEN DART

REAL IDENTITY: May Tang

POWERS: Flight. Wristbands fire explosive darts.

ORIGIN: May always wanted to be a hero like her mother, the first Golden Dart. After her mom died at the hands of the ghastly Mr. Morbid, May designed a similar costume with upgraded weapons to take down his criminal empire.

STRENGTH ◈◇◇◇◇
INTELLIGENCE ◈◈◈◇◇
SPECIAL POWERS ◈◈◇◇◇
FIGHTING SKILLS ◈◈◈◇◇

COSTUME COLORS
Why does your hero dress in a particular way? Golden Dart's brown and tan outfit shows her origins as a legacy hero. However, your hero might want to make a bold statement with bright colors, or wear dark hues to hide in the shadows at night.

CHARACTER DYNAMICS
How do your characters relate to one another? While Golden Dart may look like a blast from the past, she's a modern woman, with technological know-how and a quick wit — the opposite of Ice-Age Mammoth! There's a real culture clash when the pair meet.

NAME: SCARAB

REAL IDENTITY: Rosa Ramirez

POWERS: Super senses, gymnastic ability, tracker.

ORIGIN: Framed for crimes she didn't commit, Rosa spent months in solitary confinement. In her cell, she was bitten by mutant beetles. This caused her to develop an uncanny ability to communicate with insects. Freed, she used her super senses to track down those who framed her.

STRENGTH ◆◆◇◇◇
INTELLIGENCE ◆◆◆◇◇
SPECIAL POWERS ◆◆◇◇◇
FIGHTING SKILLS ◆◆◆◆◇

SUPERPOWERS

Your hero may be a mutant who was born with incredible powers. They may have gained powers through scientific or mystical means—even by accident! Or maybe your hero became strong and resourceful through hard work and determination.

TOP TIP

When you assemble a super team, choose heroes with diverse powers so that they each add something to the group. Not every teammate has to be strong or clever.

INSPIRATION

Nature is a great place to look for ideas for super characters. Scarab is named after a large, tough beetle. Names, powers, and costumes can be inspired by animals, plants, or even the weather!

SECRET IDENTITY

Who is your hero when they aren't fighting villains? Shellshock is an army veteran. After being betrayed by his own commanding officer, he finds it hard to trust anyone.

OVERCOMING CHALLENGES

What struggles will your characters overcome? Shellshock was paralyzed from the neck down, so he used his engineering skills to create his high-tech armor.

NAME: SHELLSHOCK

REAL IDENTITY: Roy Martin

POWERS: Wears strong defensive armor with built-in weapons and computer interface.

ORIGIN: When this gifted army engineer was injured in combat, he knew he had to do more. While his "Hardshell" tech protects troops, Roy guards his home city as an armored superhero.

STRENGTH ◆◆◆◇◇
INTELLIGENCE ◆◆◆◆◆
SPECIAL POWERS ◆◆◆◆◇
FIGHTING SKILLS ◆◇◇◇◇

STRIKE A POSE

Here are the basics for drawing a hero in a dynamic pose, ready for action.

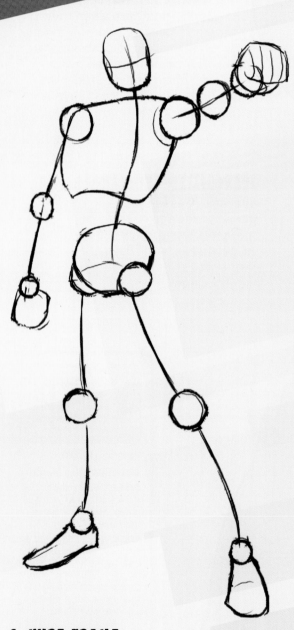 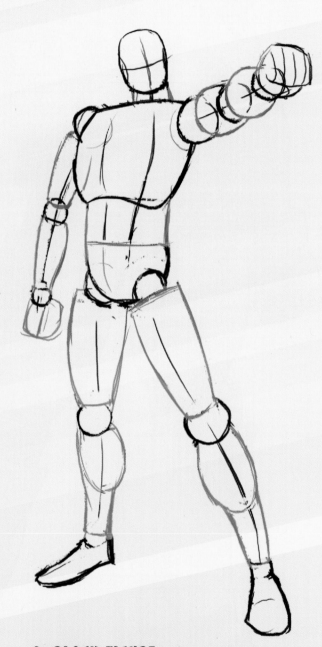

1. WIRE FRAME

Using light pencil marks, draw a simple stick figure showing your hero's pose, with circles for joints. Make the pose dramatic, but be sure that the proportions are correct.

2. BLOCK FIGURE

Use basic shapes to fill out your figure: an oval head, a rounded torso that goes in toward the waist, and cylindrical arms and legs. The figure's left arm seems short but gets wider the closer it is to the viewer. This effect is called **FORESHORTENING**.

TOP TIP

Even if your hero wears bulky armor, draw the body underneath before adding the costume to make sure they can fit inside!

3. ANATOMY

Add flesh to your hero. Replace the body blocks with more accurate anatomy, muscles, and joints. Reshape the hands and feet, adding fingers. Carefully erase your original construction lines.

4. FINISHED PENCIL SKETCHES

Now tighten your pencil sketches. Add facial features. Finally, draw costume details, including any mask, armor, weapons, and tech. You can see how Shellshock's armor encases his body.

5. INKS

Using a fine brush or pen, go over your pencil sketches, keeping the lines you want to show on the finished figure. When the ink is dry, erase your pencil lines. Notice how the ink line becomes slightly wider over the more dominant parts of the armor.

EXAGGERATE!

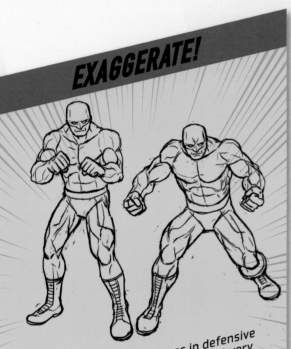

Compare these two figures in defensive poses. Figure 1 is realistic, but not very exciting. The hero looks hesitant with his limbs close together. Figure 2 is better. He has a more dramatic pose, with his shoulders back, legs wide apart, and arms reaching out. He looks confident, as a superhero should.

6. COLORS

Superheroes tend to have costumes in bold primary colors—red, blue, and yellow. Different tones emphasize the curves and shine on Shellshock's armor. His suit is clean and polished, adding to his heroic appearance.

HERO COLORS

VILLAIN COLORS

TOP TIP

Don't add too many colors to your hero or villain's costume. Two contrasting or complementary colors work best!

RACING INTO ACTION

Time to get your hero off the starting blocks. Here's how to draw a character running forward into action — heroes never run away from danger, of course!

NAME: SPRINT

REAL IDENTITY: Tyra Dupree

POWERS: Super speed.

ORIGIN: After lab assistant Tyra was exposed to a temporal-dilation experiment, she began to experience time at a different speed. To her, she is not fast — everything else is just slow!

STRENGTH ◆◇◇◇◇
INTELLIGENCE ◆◆◆◇◇
SPECIAL POWERS ◆◆◆◆◇
FIGHTING SKILLS ◆◆◆◇◇

1. Sprint leans dramatically in the direction she is racing, with her torso twisted at right angles to her waist. Her left arm is pushing forward while her left leg is behind, and vice versa for her right-hand limbs.

2. With her body leaning over, we see her shoulders and chest from above, with her torso getting thinner to her waist. Just as on a real human body, the 3D shapes used to build her form are not straight but slightly curved.

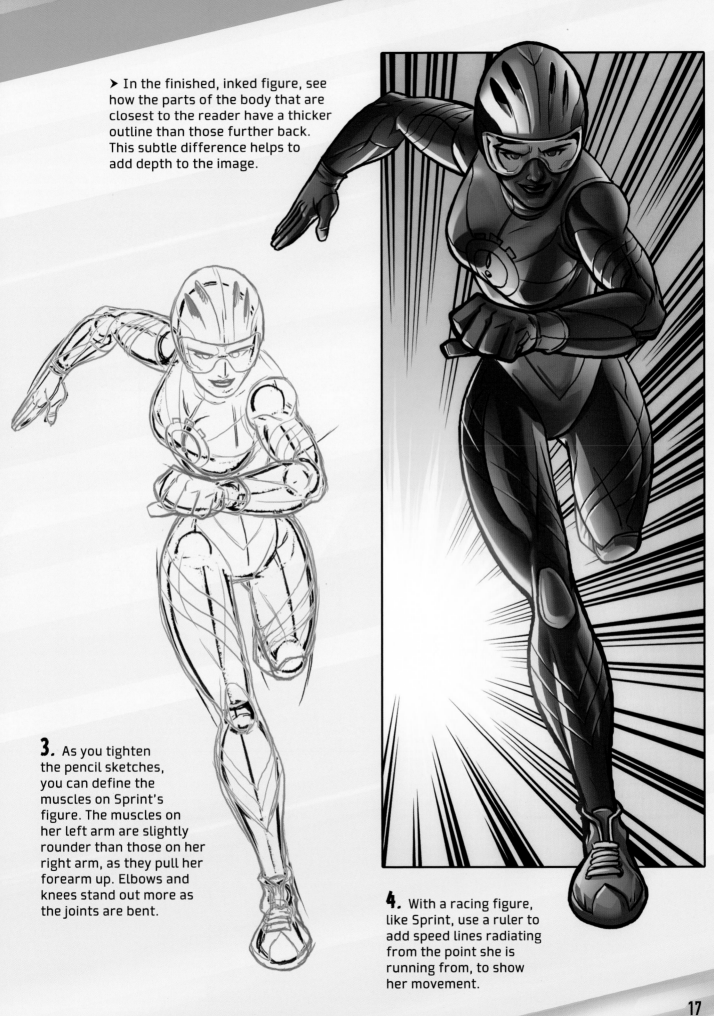

➤ In the finished, inked figure, see how the parts of the body that are closest to the reader have a thicker outline than those further back. This subtle difference helps to add depth to the image.

3. As you tighten the pencil sketches, you can define the muscles on Sprint's figure. The muscles on her left arm are slightly rounder than those on her right arm, as they pull her forearm up. Elbows and knees stand out more as the joints are bent.

4. With a racing figure, like Sprint, use a ruler to add speed lines radiating from the point she is running from, to show her movement.

TAKING OFF

How should you draw a flying character? Charge is an electrically powered hero launching himself into the stratosphere. Find out how you can make him really leap from the page.

NAME: CHARGE

REAL IDENTITY: Brad Beckerman

POWERS: Control of electricity, flight, electrical body held together by willpower.

ORIGIN: Construction engineer Brad Beckerman was caught in a freak lightning storm that disintegrated his body but left his mind intact. He now exists as an electrical charge in a high-tech containment suit.

STRENGTH	◈◈◈◇◇
INTELLIGENCE	◈◈◇◇◇
SPECIAL POWERS	◈◈◈◈◇
FIGHTING SKILLS	◈◈◇◇◇

1. Our flying hero — Charge — is propelling himself upward from a rooftop to take flight. One leg is bent as he pushes up, but the rest of his body is stretching into the sky.

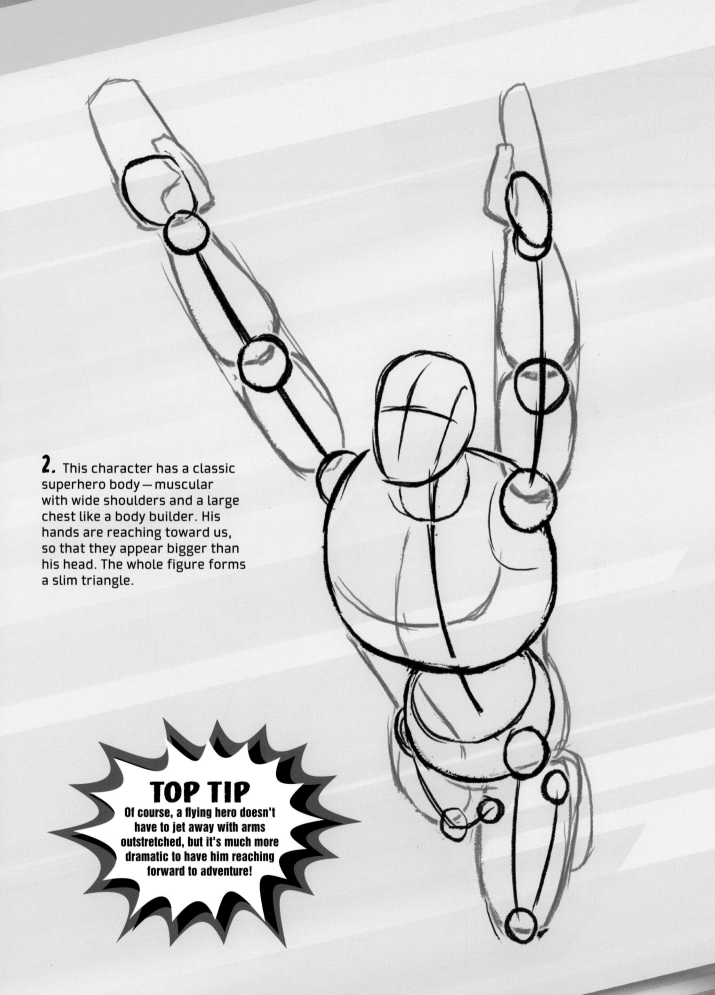

2. This character has a classic superhero body — muscular with wide shoulders and a large chest like a body builder. His hands are reaching toward us, so that they appear bigger than his head. The whole figure forms a slim triangle.

TOP TIP
Of course, a flying hero doesn't have to jet away with arms outstretched, but it's much more dramatic to have him reaching forward to adventure!

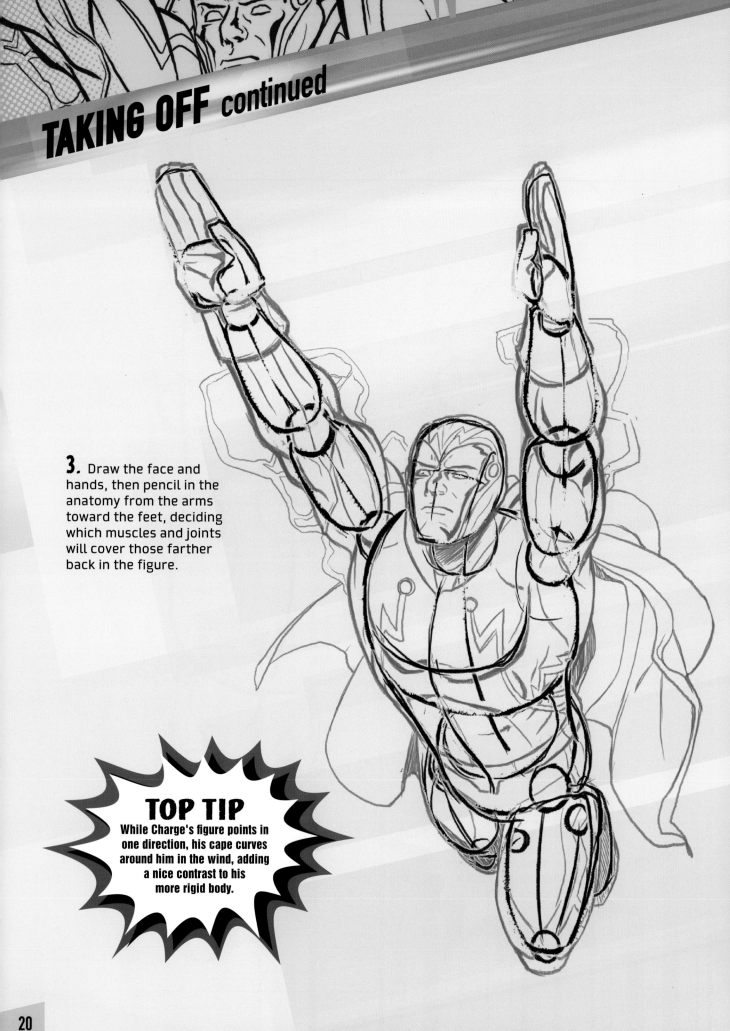

3. Draw the face and hands, then pencil in the anatomy from the arms toward the feet, deciding which muscles and joints will cover those farther back in the figure.

TOP TIP
While Charge's figure points in one direction, his cape curves around him in the wind, adding a nice contrast to his more rigid body.

4. The inked lines are much thicker around the parts of the body closest to the reader — the hands and arms. The lines get thinner toward the knees. A crackle of electrical light traces his upper body.

⌃ Charge's flowing cape ends with a curved line to show the folds in the fabric. For each fold, draw a line flowing up the cape toward where it is pinned on the hero. The line gets thinner as the fold disappears.

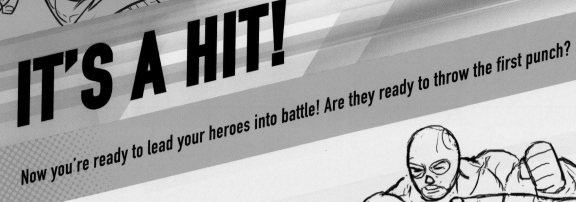

IT'S A HIT!

NAME: KNOCKOUT

REAL IDENTITY: Jamila Rice

POWERS: Absorbs kinetic energy and uses it to power explosive punches.

ORIGIN: After handling a glowing meteorite, mineralogist Rice lost the feeling in her hands as her body took on its properties of kinetic energy transferral.

STRENGTH ◆◆◆◆◇
INTELLIGENCE ◆◆◆◇◇
SPECIAL POWERS ◆◆◆◇◇
FIGHTING SKILLS ◆◆◆◇◇

➤ Here, Knockout is punching a thug, but it's not a very exciting pose. While the villain is being hit hard, you don't really feel the power of the punch. It looks like a gentle tap!

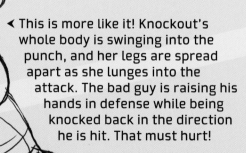

◄ This is more like it! Knockout's whole body is swinging into the punch, and her legs are spread apart as she lunges into the attack. The bad guy is raising his hands in defense while being knocked back in the direction he is hit. That must hurt!

➤ In this inked version, **MOTION LINES** have been added, so you can see the arc of Knockout's swinging punch. As you draw your fighting hero, think about how her body would twist to follow the action, with the torso and shoulders turning as she moves.

◄ A starburst effect has been added near the punch in the finished inked picture to show where Knockout's fist makes contact with the villain's chin. The finished facial expressions show Knockout's determination and her enemy's pain as he winces from the punch.

PLANNING THE PAGE

Now that you have the basics of drawing your heroes in action, it's time to plan a comic page with more than one panel. The scene shows the hero Mammoth in conflict with evil genius Automator.

◀ This is a **THUMBNAIL** — a small, rough plan of the comic page. A variety of views, from wide-open shots to close-ups, should be used on the page to make it exciting. There are six panels leading to the big event when Mammoth breaks free. The action should lead your eye toward this point.

NAME: **AUTOMATOR**

REAL IDENTITY: **Rohan Sen**

POWERS: Superior robotics engineer.

ORIGIN: Sen used his scientific genius to build a helmet that would free his mind from human inefficiency. It turned him into a ruthless monster!

STRENGTH ◆◇◇◇◇
INTELLIGENCE ◆◆◆◆◇
SPECIAL POWERS ◆◆◆◇◇
FIGHTING SKILLS ◆◆◇◇◇

The first panel is an **ESTABLISHING SHOT** to set the scene in downtown Capital City, showing Automator's machine approaching Mammoth.

Pale-blue ruled **PERSPECTIVE LINES** help the artist to draw buildings at the correct angle.

THUMBNAILS

Comic book artists use loose thumbnail sketches to plan each page. They may try several versions, with enough drama and contrast, until they are happy that the page works. Changes can be made to the page design right up to the inking stage.

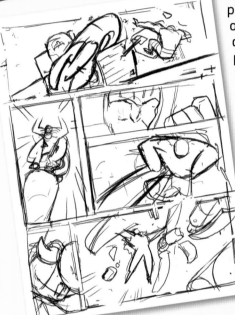

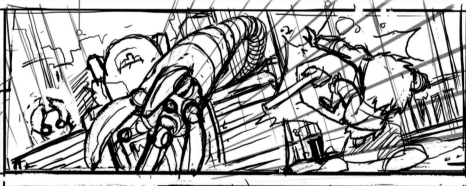

Panel 2 is a **MEDIUM SHOT** from Automator's point of view, showing all of Mammoth's body.

Panel 3 is a close-up of the evil villain.

◄ Even when there's a lot to draw, don't forget to allow space for the characters' dialogue. Speech balloons can take up about a third of the panel; they are usually placed along the top.

➤ Mammoth looks like he's going to be squashed by the machine. The view of the hero gets tighter, too, so you can feel the pressure he is under and see the struggle in his face.

➤ The finished inked page has a lot of drama, with every panel pulling you through the story. The shaded areas have been filled in black. Extra background detail has been added to some panels, along with some motion lines, but not so much that it distracts from the main action.

MAKING A SPLASH

While your comic book needs pages with lots of panels to tell the story, sometimes it's best to break out of the borders and draw a scene that fills the whole page! This is called a splash panel.

1. Capital City's finest heroes, The Vigilant, have gathered to combat the alien Amoeboid before it consumes all around it! The rough plan for this scene places the four heroes in and around the beast. Shellshock is closest to us so that he appears the largest.

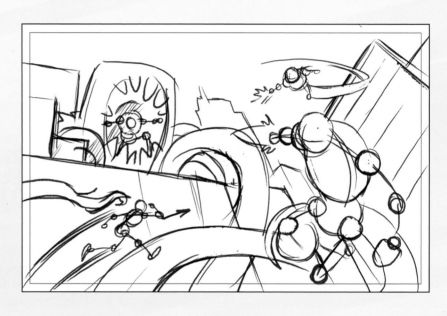

2. Ruled perspective lines show the angles of the buildings in the background. Our point of view on the action is looking up at the creature, from near ground level.

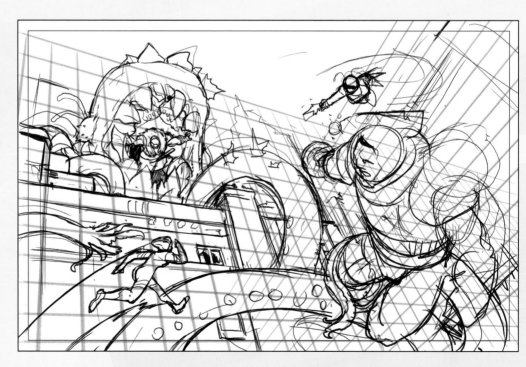

3. The pencil sketches show more clearly how the heroes are interacting with one another and the alien. While most of The Vigilant are looking at the Amoeboid and its tentacles, they should also be keeping an eye on their teammates and reacting to one another visually, not just relying on dialogue to push the story forward.

4. The final inked image draws your gaze toward the main action around the alien. Its curling tentacles contrast with the angular buildings and Shellshock's shiny armor.

BATTLEGROUND

And here's the finished battle royal in full color. Shadows are added with darker colors, giving depth to the scene and helping the monster and the champions to stand out.

THE PERFECT PLOT

What do you need to create a satisfying adventure?
Here are a few tips on writing a gripping comic book story.

TOP TIP
Give your heroes varied personalities. Even if they are powerful, they may have issues with teammates or suffer from a lack of confidence.

ACT 1. THE SETUP

Characters are introduced, and a threat appears. The first part of your story introduces the setting and main characters before something dramatic happens to lead your heroes into danger. Give the villains a good reason to cause trouble—jealousy, revenge, a troubled past, or a craving for something they don't have.

ACT 2. THE CONFRONTATION

The hero investigates and ends up in danger. The villain should appear to be a genuine threat. Heroes often lose the battle on a first attempt and have to improve or discover a new way to defeat their foe. This provides a chance for **CHARACTER DEVELOPMENT**.

ACT 3. THE RESOLUTION

The hero finds a way to escape and save the day. While planning the setup, think ahead to how your hero will escape. Don't make it obvious—say, by smashing her way out. Have your hero use her brain. The hero, and possibly the villain, should have learned something new by the end of the story.

TO BE CONTINUED!

Of course, you could always end with a **CLIFFHANGER**...and hold off Act 3 till the next issue!

GLOSSARY

ACTION LINES Lines that appear behind a moving object or person to show speed.

CHARACTER DEVELOPMENT Growth and change in a character that makes them more interesting and compelling.

CLIFFHANGER An ending of an episode that leaves the audience in suspense.

ESTABLISHING SHOT A panel that shows where the action is set.

FORESHORTENING A perspective effect that makes objects appear closer.

MEDIUM SHOT A view that shows a figure in full.

MOTION LINES Lines that illustrate the movement of an object or person.

PERSPECTIVE A way of representing three-dimensional (3D) objects in a picture.

PERSPECTIVE LINES Vertical and horizontal lines that radiate from a point or points in a drawing to create the illusion of depth.

PROPORTIONS The relative size of parts in a single object or subject.

SPEECH BALLOON A shape used in comic panels to hold character dialogue.

SYMMETRICAL Shapes on either side of an imaginary line that are mirror images of each other.

THUMBNAIL A rough small-scale sketch used for planning a page layout.

FURTHER INFORMATION

Books to read

Drawing Manga: Step by Step by Ben Krefta (Arcturus Publishing, 2013)

Stan Lee's How to Draw Superheroes by Stan Lee (Watson-Guptill, 2013)

The Super Book for Super-Heroes by Jason Ford (Laurence King, 2013)

Write and Draw Your Own Comics by Louise Stowell and Jess Bradley (Usborne, 2014)

Websites

PowerKids Press has developed an online list of websites related to the subject of this book. This site is updated regularly. Please use this link to access the list: **www.powerkidslinks.com/uca/classic**

INDEX

Published in 2018 by **The Rosen Publishing Group, Inc.**
29 East 21st Street, New York, NY 10010

CATALOGING-IN-PUBLICATION DATA
Names: Potter, William.
Title: Drawing classic heroes / William Potter and Juan Calle.
Description: New York : PowerKids Press, 2018. | Series: Ultimate comic art | Includes index.
Identifiers: ISBN 9781508154709 (pbk.) | ISBN 9781508154648 (library bound) | ISBN 9781508154525 (6 pack)
Subjects: LCSH: Heroes in art--Juvenile literature. | Figure drawing--Technique--Juvenile literature. |
    Comic books, strips, etc.--Technique--Juvenile literature.
Classification: LCC NC825.H45 P68 2018 | DDC 741.5'1--dc23

Copyright © 2018 Arcturus Holdings Limited

Text: William Potter
Illustrations: Juan Calle and Info Liberum
Design: Neal Cobourne
Design series edition: Emma Randall
Editor: Joe Harris

Manufactured in the United States of America
CPSIA Compliance Information: Batch BS17PK: For Further Information contact Rosen Publishing, New York, New York at 1-800-237-9932.